The A–Z Musings of a Tour Guide

THE A-Z MUSINGS OF A TOUR GUIDE

CHRIS MASLIN

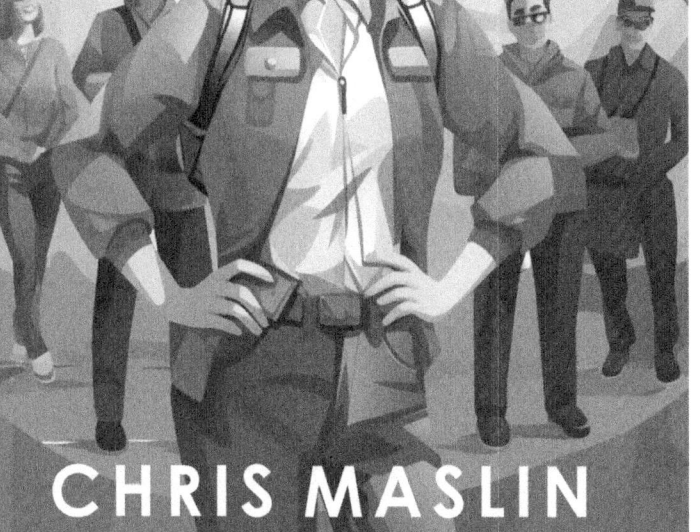

Copyright © 2023 by Chris Maslin

All rights reserved. No part of this book may be reproduced or used in any manner without written permission of the copyright owner except for the use of quotations in a book review. For more information, contact: chris.maslin@btopenworld.com

FIRST EDITION

978-1-80541-394-3 (paperback)
978-1-80541-395-0 (eBook)

Preface

Following my recovery from a hip replacement, I decided to slowly reintegrate myself back into society by securing a nice and relaxed customer service role without any stress. Unwittingly, I soon found out I had agreed to become a tour guide.

In my defence, the job description and interview had proven to be a little wayward and it was the first day's training on terrorism which gave the game away. Fortunately, I found out I wasn't the only new member of staff that had been provided with a slightly different career path than had been requested.

Naturally, every sinew in my body was communicating with my brain that I should now consider early retirement with immediate effect as I didn't manage a wink of sleep in the early weeks. Unwinding and relaxing is not so easy when you are desperately trying to learn a period of history spanning six hundred years before the next day.

What followed was an incredible journey and one which I was extremely sad to leave after the end of my initial fixed term contract. I have been fortunate to make some amazing friends along the way and I simply must share with you the perspective of a tour guide; someone many of us have, until now, simply taken for granted.

Index

- **A**   **A**necdotes 1
- **B**   **B**ees 3
- **C**   **C**ash 5
- **D**   **D**rones 7
- **E**   **E**ntrance 9
- **F**   **F**oreign Languages 13
- **G**   **G**ardens 15
- **H**   **H**igh Viz 17
- **I**   **I**nformation 19
- **J**   **J**okes 21
- **K**   **K**now-It-Alls 23
- **L**   **L**ingering 25
- **M**   **M**usical Chairs 27
- **N**   **N**ear Misses 29
- **O**   **O**pening Times 31
- **P**   **P**atience 33

Q	**Q**ueues	35
R	**R**efreshments	37
S	**S**chool Trips	39
T	**T**oilets	41
U	**U**mbrellas	43
V	**V**aping	45
W	**W**ells	47
X	**X**-Factor	49
Y	**Y**ear-Round	51
Z	**Z**ip	53

Anecdotes

A tip which I quickly learnt, to cover up the smell of my own fear, was to provide amusement to visitors, preferably not at my own expense.

Living in the uncertain post-Covid world, I found my planned training had disappeared as quickly as it had been promised, due to staff absences. Within two weeks, I was now faced with the isolated and frightening prospect of being descended upon by groups of fifty plus visitors, looking up at me expectantly for knowledge and entertainment in a Covid-secure environment.

Rather than initially focusing on and stumbling over a plethora of historical facts spanning many centuries,

I quickly started to introduce anecdotes and trusted in luck that my audiences would start to laugh.

This would not always be the case and, when my number one go-to anecdote failed, it would dawn on me too late that the group in front of me didn't actually speak or understand a word of English. Initially, this proved to be very frustrating and was often undetected by me until *after* I had finished my five-minute spiel.

Without a doubt, I have retained a fascination of where current phrases and sayings originate from and it was lovely to demonstrate these within the context of an historical setting. Please watch this space for additional literary bliss so you are not left wondering for any longer than necessary why medlar fruits are known as dog's bottoms.

Bees

Having been employed by an institution which keeps bees that produce honey for sale on site, I have grown quite fond of the little blighters.

That said, I have seen absolute chaos ensue when the bees accidentally become trapped in the visitor reception area of a property, with bumps and bruises aplenty for the fleeing visitors and staff.

Beware, however, of a few warnings and the first one is not to impress the bees with your heavily perfumed aftershave or scent as these aromas can be misleading for the bees when they are furtively working in their fragrant surroundings.

Secondly, bees are very much a victim of the country's booming house market and, should there be piling or digging nearby, please give them a wide berth. I have witnessed some bees stealing from neighbouring hives and some were subsequently placed on the naughty step off site for several weeks to reflect on their behaviour and to further consider their actions.

Thirdly, and perhaps most irritating of all, was observing some people attempting to scoop up the bees for takeaway and placing them in jars under the justification that it's a free country; no funny anecdotes for them.

Cash

I am a lover of cash and feel vain and richer when I am carrying a wad of it around with me in my wallet, but post-Covid, many companies are still phasing this out as presumably it's easier and more secure to be cashless.

Many times, I had the misfortune to explain to customers that cash was no longer permitted and I learnt a valuable lesson: duck!

I do, however, empathise with those overseas visitors who have carefully planned their visits by carrying the right currency and it was often not a pretty sight when they realised it was card only.

Personally, I do not see the value of fifty pound notes anymore either and I wish you good luck spending those at the moment. Not only is there potential forgery but no employee really wants to dispense all their change from the cashier's till after completing one transaction.

Whilst it's an evolving world right now, I recommend having a card back-up with you always. That said, using American Express in a small retail outlet will prove about as likely to succeed as when you ask for change from a fifty pound note.

Drones

An unfortunate necessity for the difficult times we live in, but next time you see a small personal drone hovering above a private area, will you please spare a thought for the poor and unfortunate tour guide?

It's clear that some people have far too much time on their hands and their sole purpose in the morning is to become a focal point of attention by flying their drone over a public space, armed with their oversized body camera.

Naturally, I concede these devices also have their commercial uses. However, I draw the line when individuals are filming public areas that may include children.

Should you approach the "pilot", then you are smugly greeted with a multitude of "I know my rights" statements and they often implore you to call the authorities so they can be promoted further into the spotlight.

What really would help the beleaguered tour guide is for these delightful sorts to stay at home and play a nice game of Scrabble instead and perhaps ask the bee kidnappers to pop round to also join them safely indoors.

Entrance

A word to drive terror into a tour guide's shift as you observe the masses of people merrily trotting down the path towards you in front of the entrance to the property. Not only are you a human crowd barrier, but you do not know until everyone has reached you quite what you are dealing with.

Dogs are definitely worth a mention too as you often see a look of horror on people's faces when they realise their beloved pets are not allowed into the actual property with them.

Two or more people can easily resolve this situation if you are not distracted by the dog's whining for the person who has entered, but solo travellers are somewhat different. I have seen ridiculously small dogs tucked into people's rucksacks and overcoats when they have realised that dog sitting is not an official responsibility of a tour guide. Well, not yet anyway.

Everyone likes value for money and wishes to listen to a short historical introduction, or do they? To an outsider, I am sure it's quite amusing watching some members of the public try to duck under a tour guide's arm when they are pointing at certain historical aspects of the property.

No empathy or consideration is shown to how, later that evening, the tour guide will be rubbing Deep Heat into their aching shoulders.

Personally, I liked to provide a brief overview before people entered the property and issue the salient health and safety warnings. As time progressed, I learnt not to bang my own head on the low ceilings, although this did provide a fantastic visual demonstration of what you're *not* meant to do.

What I did enjoy, however, was observing married couples on the way in when they had clearly had an earlier argument on whether they should visit the property. The loving smile from the interested party was a terrific complement to the dagger-like stare from the other when they realised they would also have to listen to some historical facts, when clearly they would rather have been down the pub or watching cricket in the first place.

Foreign Languages

An exceptionally long time ago, I studied A-Level French and I didn't realise that many years later I would be searching through my fading memory to see what I could remember and whether the basics applied to other languages too.

Many times, I would entertain large groups of overseas visitors and you would feel relieved when they had their own interpreter with them.

That was until you realised you would have to deliver a slow and staggered presentation in English, waiting for the interpreter to do their stuff.

Slowly, you would become increasingly hot and sweaty as you felt like a complete spanner and then it would dawn on you that you were also being filmed, just to add to your day.

Without doubt, I am sure I have become an internet sensation in some countries because, as hard as you try, you can never completely hide from those intrusive cameras and unwittingly ruining visitors' camera shots.

Gardens

A lovely shift on a tour guide's rota where you can mingle with customers and relax away from the expectant masses, you would think.

Bins seemed pretty straightforward concepts until now and the "Keep Britain Tidy" slogan was an easy message, I thought. Upon reflection, maybe it should read:

- A space is within the bin for you to place your rubbish
- Not on top or by the side, but actually inside the bin

- Thanks for cluttering up the surrounding area but could you please actually use the space inside the bin, if you really don't mind

Naturally, everyone loves the odd apple or pear to keep the doctor at bay, although where is the fun in picking a nice rosy one from a sturdy accessible branch in favour of climbing up a tree and causing as much damage as possible?

There's time afterwards for the guide to have a spot of relaxation on a bench once they have removed all the litter from the bench first and placed it within the neighbouring bin only a few yards away, following the carefully worded instructions.

High Viz

A tour guide should be as visible as possible and I am sure you have seen the wonderful array of bright colours that can be on display following expensive and researched designs by the branding team.

Don't be concerned by a little bit of sweat or oversizing issues as you really cannot expect visitors to read a sign that says "This Way". Tour guide discomfort must always be of paramount importance.

Notwithstanding the visibility requirements, sign-posting is especially important and embellishes the experience when you are frequently asked for the way out: "Please follow the sign in front of you which says exit."

The presence of the tour guide also provides alerts for those visitors looking to cause destruction.

When planning their ever-so-funny mayhem, it can often be quite difficult for some lovely people to improvise when the colourful tour guide decides to follow them around the property until they leave, without satisfying their most amusing urges to wreck the place first.

Information

A short time after the visitor has entered the property, there is quite rightly a large volume of information available, either on story boards or directly from the lovely tour guide.

I would, however, like to spare a moment's thought for those customers who look in astonishment when they see a sign encouraging the scanning of a QR code and downloading an interactive app.

Rapidly approaching the age where new technology has started to become challenging, I do afford myself a wry smile when I see the look of bemusement on some visitors' faces and the sheer incomprehension at the fact they're being invited to use their mobile phone.

Sometimes, visitors will backtrack and review their hasty decision not to have purchased a guidebook at the front desk, and they subsequently decide not to take a chance that their guide may not satisfy their sudden and unexpected thirst for knowledge.

To be honest, I do prefer the personal touch and it's nice to see reliance is still there on individuals, rather than robots. For the moment anyway.

Jokes

A tool I have often relied on in addition to my anecdotes, and my personal critics would accuse me of having an overactive thyroid.

Feedback on the whole was positive and I achieved enormous personal satisfaction when I helped embellish a person's visit.

One customer enquired whether I knew of any coffee shops she could leave her mother at whilst she visited a neighbouring attraction. Without hesitation, I suggested she leave her mother in a castle dungeon. With huge relief, I observed a large smile and laughter appear in double quick time.

Similarly, I threatened to call the RSPCA when a slightly inebriated customer was unable to keep hold of a recently acquired plastic duck and I am pleased to report this also did not generate a negative review on TripAdvisor.

There is much to be said for building good public relations and this is without doubt one of the most enjoyable aspects of being a tour guide.

Know-It-Alls

As your experience in the role grows, you quickly learn to spot these from afar, wondering why they actually purchased a ticket. Usually, these will be those visitors who have entered just before closing time and it's a shame they weren't smart enough to realise they could have arrived earlier.

I had a motto that I would let the first contradiction by a customer go, the second one would be a gracious "we'll have to agree to disagree" and the third and last one was a look at my watch and definitely time for their exit stage left, mentioning time was moving on.

Just to clarify to anyone who has always wondered, no, you don't get a discount for entering a property late!

Mindful that customers pay my wages, I would gladly not get paid on these occasions as these individuals can ruin a day out for many.

Their often snail-like and funeral march from the property leaves the guide in fear they will do a U-turn and ask yet another rhetorical question and it's only when the door is firmly closed that you can start to feel safe.

Lingering

A tour guide will not be the best paid individual on the planet and benefits can be surprisingly lacking. I was also surprised as to how tired I would become, although the fresh air was probably largely responsible for this.

During the day, time will fly by, although when you are flagging at the end of your shift, the escorting of customers from the property does present a challenge, especially when you have to smile and be cheerful at the same time.

My plea to those of you wishing to visit a tourist attraction is to consider the staff and please don't assume they will be rewarded with shift allowances and overtime; all they will receive is the opportunity to sit in even more traffic on their way home.

You may also be shocked to learn that customer tips are not frowned upon by tour guides and it's quite a galling sight watching a tip meant for you being inserted into the coffers of the institutional gratuity box.

Once the tour guide arrives home, a warm bath and quick drink is followed by the opportunity to do exactly the same thing again tomorrow.

Unfortunately, it's not just the Know-It-Alls who like to dawdle and once I made the schoolboy error of stopping off at the local pub on the way home. This was not a clever move on my part as many visitors also had the same idea and I then had the wonderful opportunity to answer many additional questions, without any pay whatsoever.

Musical Chairs

A well-run institution will see their guides rotated on a regular basis and you may often see them in different areas of the attraction, resembling the comedy sketch showing just one person working for the same employer.

Not only will this keep the knowledge of the tour guide fresh, but it will also provide visitors with the opportunity to use the "didn't I see your brother in another room?" gag. Remember, a tour guide must keep smiling gracefully.

On the flip side, this can also become a distinct barrier to avoiding the Know-It-Alls referred to earlier when you have the absolute honour of serving them again in another section of the property.

The imagination runs wild and it may be paranoia on my part, but I would swear that you can see a vicious grin appear on the faces of the Know-It-Alls as they approach you for the second time.

With experience, a tour guide can learn to anticipate these clashes following an in-depth study of their rota for the day and become quite adept in needing a comfort break or tying shoelaces at opportune moments.

Near Misses

A complete bane of my life as, when you have an accident, you must complete a Near Miss Report and this was a prominent feature of my early head-banging fetish I had developed.

Let's address the elephant in the room first. Why aren't they called Direct Hit Reports? Answers on a postcard, please.

One of my dear friends reported an extra-large head bang by yours truly on a low beam. From that moment onwards they became fondly known to me as "Snitchy" as there really is nothing worse than filling these forms out, especially at the end of the day.

When asked by management how this could be avoided in the future, I can with hindsight now see how my suggestion may not have been construed as helpful when I asked them to pay for a surgeon to make me shorter.

These wonderful inventions also extend to visitors and they do not only apply to unfortunate first-aid experiences. They can also be filled out for when apples nearly fall on your head, a bee flies too close to you and for when you become too warm in the sun. Global warming has a lot to answer for.

Opening Times

A firm runs a business, advertises when it opens and closes, and customers attend during these hours. What could be any easier?

It's quite extraordinary how some people will travel considerable distances to visit your attraction, standing patiently outside for up to an hour before you open. There is a clue on the noticeboard and indeed on the internet but clearly this is insufficient for many.

Not deterred, we'll be asked if they can quickly pop round early and presumably think we can order some more guides through a TARDIS, bright-eyed and bushy-tailed.

The fun and games really start when visitors appear well after the advertised closing times and you hear the classic "it's my only chance to visit and I have always wanted to come here".

Refusal most certainly does offend but a tourist attraction does have to draw a line somewhere.

Patience

A quality you must possess in abundance when dealing with the public and unfortunately, this often doesn't always extend the other way.

During the heatwave, our clearly selfish priority was to stay cool and remain alive and this involved copious quantities of shade and water.

Erecting a temporary pergola seemed like a very clever idea to stop us from resembling panting dogs, although the purpose seemed lost on the visitors who tutted disdainfully and said their pictures were being ruined by such an eyesore.

The pergola was also deemed to have been the wrong colour and sometimes I do wonder if Covid has left us with a legacy of being a bunch of moaners.

Upon reflection, should the pergola not have been erected then I'm sure complaints would have been made about the sun and there would have been a backlog of Near Miss Reports to complete.

Queues

A start to your day like no other when visitors moan they have been outside waiting for so long, which often equates to at least two whole minutes. Just wait until I inform you that you can't use cash, madam.

Crowd management was definitely a key skill and I could often redirect human traffic without them realising this and referrals to health and safety could have their uses.

Having listened to various concerns expressed at the door, you then have to contend with ticketing and I vividly remember a group of twenty spontaneous overseas visitors descending on me at the same time. The system I used was a little overly complicated and it could take a few minutes to process each individual ticket; I could not calculate exactly how many tuts I received during the processing, but well over a hundred.

Just as customers are safely exiting the property, there is also the chance to stop off for a little retail therapy and it's amazing how a long queue can suddenly appear when you have tried to explain no cash, no AmEx and no, I do not accept fifty pound notes.

Should you be feeling really lucky, your rota has been engineered so you can receive more tuts from the same group you served earlier on ticketing when later covering a shift in retail.

Refreshments

I knew this would be trouble from when the infamous customer of a large restaurant chain historically sued the company as there was no warning on a coffee lid stating the contents may be hot.

Looking to resolve that obviously major issue, the teas and coffees where I worked are served in a copiously worded container with a folding lid. In truth, I imagine they were probably designed to stop those naughty customers from spilling their drinks after they had smuggled them inside the property undetected, alongside their dogs.

Staff operating these facilities should be commended for their resilience as personally I would struggle with the challenge of looking at drinks and sumptuous refreshments without sampling the offerings on a regular basis to make sure they were still fresh.

"The customer is always right" in my opinion is a complete load of twaddle nowadays and social media platforms encourage poor reviews. Should you pay two pounds for a half-decent cup of coffee, you may complain that you did not receive five-star refreshments, and if you pay four pounds, then it's overpriced.

What should be important is that you have had the opportunity to refuel and continue about your day and should you decide not to, it's your personal choice and should not be regarded as news to share with the world.

School Trips

Most certainly a candidate for a book of its own from the sheer terror these two words can bring to your day.

A tour guide will nervously check their rota to see when they are on entrance and should this coincide with school trips, I would strongly recommend to others they develop a sudden migraine because one will certainly be on the way down to you.

Despite the best intentions of the guide, any speech will be brutally ignored and, if you are lucky, you may receive eye contact from two of a group of thirty. Once the speech is over, then it's everybody for themselves as you desperately try to prevent highly precious and valuable artefacts from being taken for a walk.

"Is that real?" was the most common question I experienced as I saw a multitude of hands reaching out to manhandle everything in sight. That said, I did manage to achieve a tick off my personal bucket list when I stopped my speech and then asked two overly loud children to finish their conversation and share the content with the rest of the group.

The refreshments and gift shop are two of the most wonderful diversionary tactics for the redirection of stampeding children, provided you have first checked on the rota these are not on your next shift.

Toilets

A key part of any establishment and this was also a source of increased aggravation for those customers who decided not to check admission prices first and then decided they would not pay to come in upon arrival.

Following their realisation that all toilets are inside the property (and the other side of the pay desk), this really does become a battlefield.

This causes immense discontent from prospective visitors and the immediate desire from a tour guide to be located anywhere else within the property at that point.

I'm a firm advocator of the saying "you need to go when you need to go" but unfortunately, on many occasions, visitors have used this opportunity to sneak around the attraction for nothing. With the best will in the world, there are not the financial resources or legal permissions to provide an escort service.

Naturally, we are seen as the enemy on this occasion, but a little research and planning of a visitor's day wouldn't go amiss. Please also note the toilets have the same closing times as the front gate; you have been warned.

Umbrellas

A fantastic invention and very much a necessity for both visitors and tour guides, although this can also ruin camera shots.

It's pretty clear that, whilst this country has successfully launched people into space, we have not quite invented that ideal bucket for a multitude of wet umbrellas to be stored in.

Naturally, shaking an umbrella dry creates yet more opportunities for Near Miss Reports from the resultant slippery floors.

Perhaps one hazard many people don't foresee is that it's amazingly easy to drop an umbrella with cold hands and I once had a visitor do this, causing the umbrella to explode open.

With a degree of fortune, the protruding spikes came within an inch of my crown jewels and I am not sure any Near Miss Report would have covered that eventuality. Fortunately, nervous and relieved laughter won the day and first aid was not required.

Vaping

I used to be a heavy smoker and indeed still use nicotine gum; society is not so forgiving on vaping, however.

One of my privileges of rank was to inform people that smoking and vaping were not permitted, especially those who allegedly couldn't read the signs properly.

Personally, I have empathy for vapers who are trying very hard to kick the habit, especially as smoking is so unaffordable now.

Shops are under strict instructions not to have smoking devices or cigarettes on display, but it does seem an incredible leap of faith to say this will deter smokers from buying them.

What still puzzles me is why there cannot be vaping zones in open spaces away from other people. Please also send answers on a postcard to me on that one.

Wells

A well is a great feature and everybody loves a good peer down the hole; a quid please for every time I have been asked how deep it goes.

Naturally, the lid of a well can accumulate water and dirt and I remember a very rude young man staring at me coldly telling me to clean it so he could see down it properly.

Resisting my temptation to upend the individual and insert him into the hole, I politely declined.

Tutting followed as expected and following the rude hands-on-hips glare, I whispered quietly that by cleaning the well he would be able to see the other rude children at the bottom who had asked me to clean it previously.

Wishing to cap off a perfect day, I then showed tremendous empathy and understanding to a disabled gentleman by the well and, unable to access the property, we discussed his pending medical operation.

You very much enjoy these interactions with visitors and, having undergone a similar procedure and published an orthopaedic surgery guide myself, I was able to converse knowledgeably with him. Just as he was being escorted away, he told me I should also do what his surgeon had told him to do: lose weight. Thank you so much and please do come again soon.

X-Factor

A quality that most certainly applies to a tour guide with one exception: there is no audition, just misleading imprisonment.

I had repeatedly dodged presentations throughout my career until a friend of mine pointed out to me that I was doing it for a living and, whilst I didn't stand on a stage in front of four judges, it was certainly the next best thing.

Thankfully, Covid may now be on the retreat and mask wearing may soon become a thing of the past, but this is another example of the enormous trials and tribulations of a tour guide. I do, however, miss the opportunity a mask used to afford me to conceal my facial expressions.

What you should remember, however, is that, unlike performers, it's not one performance every week or so, but a tour guide must deliver their own rendition every single day.

You should also bear in mind that when visiting a property, you are perfectly entitled to bring any troubles you have with you; this is not a luxury afforded to a tour guide.

Year-Round

At most attractions, they will continue to present their offerings all year round and it's occurred to me that visitors like to be commended on travelling in poor weather conditions and for coping with extreme temperatures.

Not wishing to sound very self-centred, I do, however, feel it would be nice for empathy to be shown towards a brightly coloured individual stood in front of them.

Personally, I can't stand driving in icy conditions and we have the added bonus of driving in the early hours to make sure all is well for entry.

Whilst there are, I am sure, tour guides who also love aquaplaning to work, just a simple enquiry about their welfare may be most appreciated.

Zip

Energy is a core requirement of being a tour guide and you cannot just breeze through a day of being tired or just not feeling it as you can so often do within an office.

The lunch hour is also quite a strange concept as, if you are lucky, you will get thirty minutes and then often ten of those minutes can disappear when you are walking to and from your brief sanctuary; lack of punctuality is not an option.

Should you wish to upset a fellow tour guide, then you can easily accomplish this goal by appearing late to relieve their shift so they can go to lunch; these minutes are never recovered.

This guide has, I hope, provided you with an informative and satirical insight into the challenging life of a tour guide.

Without any doubt whatsoever, I honestly do recommend that you give it a go at some point in your life, perhaps brandishing a copy of this guide to give to some of the more difficult and challenging visitors that may await you.

Printed in Great Britain
by Amazon